~~ The Mystery
of Everything
Everywhere ~~

Thank you Zoe Zoe for the cover painting.

Morgan Drolet

Alessandra Rizzotti

Shawn Sullivan

~~ MORGAN DROLET ~~

Lightning shook windows and
thunder
thunder
thunder
zigzagwandering
across
eyes across night
Pull up a chair—pull it up
Way way up
Then sit deep deep deeeper
init
Watch the sounds and sights watch 'em
There's nothing to look for in a rainstorm
unless
you don't have a dry   spot
A popcorn of thunder
shimmies through the space between
I will sit as long as—-
Well as long
as I will
Crickets
have moved in this fall
Ask anyone
They'll say
"Sure have been a lotta crickets this year"
Like real life farm talk
They're right, sure have been
Crickets, at least these,
What ones are in my apartment,
They're vocal as hell—especially
When the lights go out
The thunder or maybe the lightning or maybe the ambiance
Seems to have quieted them for now.......

Crickets crickets

crickets

Today could be the day I die
Or the first day of the beginning of my decline
Lately I've been thinking that
Like, every day, I start off by saying
Thinking,
To myself
Maybe I won't survive the day
Or maybe it's the night I won't survive
Or maybe I will and maybe
I'll survive tomorrow too
Ever since I can remember, people
have been telling me
Be careful
Or today you might die
If I eat peanuts I could die
If I have an asthma attack, or get hit by a car again....
But now
Every day I think
I wonder if today I'll die
I think it used to scare me, maybe
And I wanted to make sure I was living
Living right
And I kept trying to figure how to do that
But know I just think, maybe I'll die today
And it just makes me feel safe
I've always been most calm in severe turbulence
There's something about out of my control that appeals to me
I wonder if death thinks of me as often

If I'm ever going to change my name
Are you?
Well I don't know
Don't know what the future holds/but
If it do
I'm just going to change it to (whatever) but with a Mrs. at the end

Whatever Whatever Mrs.

Cuz it seems dumb that I can't be a missus and
Also that people only ever think to put the missus at the front

I wouldn't be doing it for any progressive reason or to make any
meaningful statement

Just to be contrary
I'm thinking of living my life like a
Samurai
of contrarian ideas

But then I remember that my main goal is to not seek fulfillment
so it turns back into a funny idea I'll forget about
But now it's written down

Dan

He seemed old
Small and old like a scrap of leather
I seemed young
In ways I wasn't young and in the same ways he wasn't old
Maybe it's too hard to explain
why I remember him so often
these past (shoot) twenty (almost) years
I remember a body made of inflexible joints and
Taught
Screwed up tight with speed muscles
Fingers of smashed dirty nails as hats atop swollen (arthritic) knucks
He rode a bike and had a wolf he'd made a dog out of
They looked just like each other
He had a woman
They both had a nasty way of dealing with their relationship
Both sick with different things all the time
She couldn't work
But Dan could always put in a full day of manual labor while smoking his
rolled cigs
We'd eat Carl's Jr. for lunch
He'd tell us some crazy story about being bit by a bunch of brown recluse
in Arizona
where he was from
where he did construction
and he was always going back to the desert for vague reasons
One day he had prostate cancer
the next week he didn't
I think I looked down on him then
I think I thought there was magnificence in store for me and I would never
end up like him
weird and wild and old
Now I'm still not as old as he was but already I can respect him more
Not that he deserves respect necessarily
I don't know if he was a good person
But I understand better now how people can just wind up somewhere down
the road

it's almost 11 am and i'm listening to the scottish band silly wizard they're rockin out one of those celtic instrumental pipe jams they're rocking it so hard that the cricket who lives in the living room is full blown chirpin at max speed and he usually doesn't chirp during the day trying to keep up with these scottish dudes in 1978 and i'm just sitting on the couch with my dog in a brand new 2021 listening to past people communicate with present animals and i think my dog might be oblivious to all of it or maybe it's so obvious to him that it's no big deal cuz he's not a stoned human who overthinks things

Something that will get you in trouble with almost anyone at least in Los
Angeles is to say that art isn't important

I don't know why, but it really rubs people the wrong way

Even if the person you say it to is always judging whether things are
deserving of the moniker of art

Even if you say something like, I just think there are more important things in
life

Boy watch out—yer only digging yerself deeper

It's really always better to keep yer opinions to yerself

a soft knock at the door
soft so much that i hardly noticed
then again
definitely a knock
go to the door
open the wood door to reveal another closed door
a screen—for screening what filters over the threshold
the small porch
a person speaking low
mumble blanket mumble or a sheet mumble
i am taken by surprise
i try to parse what is being said but
as i said, surprised
close the door
ask the lady on the couch   he's asking for a blanket
take this one
maybe 20 seconds total had passed since he knocked to when he was gone
with the blanket
it's odd how disoriented i feel when the world comes knocking at my door
how the illusion of pasteurization can fade
odd how easy it is to forget
the world can swallow me up in a breath
the world is constantly swallowing people up
and sometimes spitting them back out

One time I tried to make someone understand me   but   First.   I tried to
think about

Me. My self from as many different angles as possible and   Then I
thought about all the different ways to explain all the different things
that I Thought

I became—well I was spinning
from thinkin
g about it—really spinning wildly like freak out and I couldn't even maybe feel
my hands or remember what hands like
mine feel like ? .
I can almost remember what it's like to have hands and So I.   just
keepgoing to pre- t
end everything is fine and eventually it is.

My hands are mine again and I can't
remember when they didn't
feel like me
but now I don't need to explain myself to anyone   I decide to keep
my mouth   Shut

We might be moving
out of the city—
already left Hollywood proper a few years back
in favor of the cheaper seats in NoHo
Now we're aiming for cheaper still
this move runs counter to everything I believed in five years ago
hell, even two years ago I was hesitant to move to here
Now we're looking at places like
Lake Hughes
Fillmore
Frazier Park
the country basically
California country
of which I have experience camping in but not so much like day to day
And like I said, this is unlike the near past me
I never even knew about nature 'til last year and now I can't shut up about it
always telling people how nature's the answer to our troubles
indigenous ways and respect for all things
corporations are a scourge
But look at me, going on about it to you
you've heard all that shit before
You even have your life all figured out
Well,
I'm still working things out on my end, but
some future awaits me
Maybe one day
in a snowy land of California hillbillies you'll see me
standing in the yard
looking as lost and out of place as I am write now

I can be instantly anything
but usually I'm not
Even when the doors and windows are wide open I am
Generally Content   To
stray not much past the porch
these days
those days   It doesn't matter to me
How I spend my time anymore
my time spends me   And that's cool

It sounds terrible   But
often, when
I think of things I'm grateful for
I just fall asleep after only thinking a few things
I think of the things in bed
at night
think of them and try my hardest   to be grateful
I feel good sometimes
and sometimes not
and sometimes I just fall asleep   which I'
m always grateful for

~~ ALESSANDRA RIZZOTTI ~~

Surviving

She was the petal and the thorn
On the ventilator
Not yet with a high school diploma
Dreams of spirituality, a living wage
A scattered brain
Made it hard to make any of that possible
And now this

Her parents cleaned buildings daily,
Working harder than
quarantined suits
She was a part of the percentage
needing plasma privilege

Life more valuable
than she deemed herself to be
Remembered more for 15 hospitalizations
than for 10 months surviving abuse
More for oscillation
than for two years without a suicide attempt
More for bloody noses
than for two weeks spent in rehab

Here's to hoping she'll survive,
at least in the afterlife
I'm grateful I got to witness
the many wins before the fall

The last card she pulled
from a deck of affirmations was
"hope is the conduit of miracles"
Here's to hoping the universe
has her back

Dying

When new shifts occur
You wonder if it will all go to shit
Or you look at it like a rebirth
Sun in Cancer,
Moon in Libra,
Scorpio rising,
Which just means
Cozy, emotional,
Nesting
Secret
Finding balance
In the chaos of
Loss

It started with a mother dying
The only mother
Pushed
Across the city
In a wheelchair
From hospice to hospice
Her breath suddenly gone
Passed through a pipe
The cacophony of ambulances
Ready to elevate
One star
To global extinction

And then the others started dying off
Like zombies walking
Through a ditch
One after another
Teaching nothing
But the inevitable
Life was meaningless
Without mother

Falling and Rising

Her eyes like puddles
Sorrow, searching,
Asking for deep connection
Through lies
Fostered by Inner darkness
Smoking through the nostrils of a dragon
Sitting on a rolling walker

I imagined her instead
On a throne
Making commands
Of minions
With blasts of light from her hands
Rising from the walker
Wings of sharp metal spread
Into oblivion

The helplessness
Suddenly nothing but an
Illusion
Her every fear of falling from
An opportunity to expand

Collecting

His name, a patch of grey particles
Collected on a mantle
Needing to be swept up
With lemon scent
Bathing with a bucket
As if he was a floor
I imagined him as if he was never
Lit on fire
A cowboy hat
Chewing tobacco
A chestnut horse
Making friends with Indians
He had wanted to be

One long fingernail
Synthetic hair woven into a balding head
Sunken cheeks from missing teeth
Claiming he had been beaten
Playing victim was easier than imagining
10 of his own
I sometimes wondered if he was a
Slown down murderer
Something eerie about someone who never cries
Who claims he has nothing then can afford everything
His smell reminded me of my father
Urine, deceit, rotting organs
A wet puppy, cologne, and sage

Bailing

Activism was a ruse
Identification with which she swallowed pain
If she could somehow change the system
The system wouldn't collapse within her
A brain so brilliant, full of ideas
Yet none that could come to fruition
Her babies never truly hers
Only figments of bad choices
The prostitution for survival
The denial pungent

Across the country she travelled
For justice that could never be
Delusions made her responsible for millions of dollars
Bailing out gutter rats wrongfully accused
Instead of focusing on the tasks
She needed to take
To hold her baby's hand again

Hiding

The quiet silence of hiding
As a teenager
Using humor to mask pain
Hair dye, hoodies, piercings, skateboards
Gained weight, suits of armor
Screams, locked doorways
Rebelling to feel one inch of something
An attitude of deflection
Just to tell the world
Things suck inside
And no, I can't tell you anything

<u>Scathing</u>

Imagine three clowns
Three stupids
Who's on first?
The child is blamed by the adult for not doing the thing the adult should have
done for the other adult
Sigh
Really destructive
Toxic
Constant jabs towards the child like: "What's wrong with you?"
Projection
Lots of unresolved bullshit
Totally ineffective
Anyways
One day somehow
The child ends up leaving the two stupids
And so now you have two stupids fighting one another over things that will
never resolve
The friction causes a literal fire in the home
And so now you have a mess
That the child has to clean up
Two stupids charred to death
By their own bullshit
The child the only one left,
Scathed by the remains

Capitulating

Oh I surrendered
The moment I heard
Stage 4
Not the movie studio kind
Not the theater kind
No, just the regular old cancer kind
The stage before the end
Every fall or wince, a chance
To enjoy the small pleasures
To drive without a license
To go to a racetrack and feel one last rumble
To find a missing son
To grieve a broken heart
Every moment
A blessing twixt with pain

Avoiding

The number one thing most people do
Is avoid pain
Three deaths later
And still the pain sat
Like rotten fruit
Waiting to be thrown out
Composted
Turned into some sort of meaning
She hadn't found yet

A chance came to live more clearly
The amount of tears it took
The amount of numbing out it took
To just know
Those deaths
Weren't all her fault
One day, she actually said
She didn't push them

Leaving

Leaving comes in many forms
As in walking out a door
Finding a new job
Deciding a relationship is over
Thoughts becoming other thoughts
Organs not functioning in the body anymore

So far I've been able to make decisions about leaving
Maybe it's because
That someone or something is
No longer serving me anymore
I'm bored
I need more
I need less
I'm at capacity

I would hope the same thing happens when I die
Maybe my organs will just decide for me
That this disease is not worth it anymore
That that accident was just too brutal
That the point of being here is lost
And yet, some of the above is not
Totally within my control

Not everything is a choice
Not everything is a decision
A lot of things are happenstance
A lot of things are somehow random
A lot of things are the results of other things
A lot of things are mysteries

~~ SHAWN SULLIVAN ~~

A Standard Hyper-contextualized Existence
a.k.a. What Isn't of Deepest Significance?

Our shower drain is clogged and I was the last

One of us to put in a call about this tremendous

Problem that irritates me. The clog manifests

About once a year and still my seemingly-deranged

Roommate will shower for a half hour or longer,

Which illustrates how my roommate makes

Decisions differently than I do, and is a potential

Bad influence on me in significant ways. Although

Everyone is human I remember, after I remind

Myself again. And if he makes the call this time.

My roommate is showering and I am writing this

Poem after having seized the opportunity to sip

An energy drink while facing the living room

Windows alone, apparently. I live attached to my

Roommate's one-bedroom apartment, with a shared

Bathroom beside my messy, cluttered studio, and

The living room is my roommate's TV lair he will

Return to soon, after his long-ass afternoon shower.

Something Like an Explosion But Not Exactly, Although I'm in Too Much of a Hurry to Stop and Further Explain

I keep suspecting that when I reach the pearly gates Saint Peter
Might ask me if I watched enough Indonesian movies, and I
Must be prepared to tell him that I tried my damn hardest
To watch as many movies as I could. The best life is many lives,

So watch many movies about other lives, since you only live once:
Sheer logic. Every time I begin writing I end up writing about myself.
All of my writing is the continuing adventures of my search for an
Escape from an existential labyrinth. I feel trapped with my life and

I write myself escape routes. I won't die thinking about grammar! I'll die
In an existential maze, with the real exit right around the corner, almost
Made it. I was just about to watch Denis Villeneuve's *Arrival* but I died
First, oops. No one cares, and I've never committed desperation without

Intentional humor. Never having not been hysterical, I'm used to it.
I'm singing my farewell song as this flaming ship sinks. And what do
The flames matter to a sinking ship? Approaching my end, here I go!
What's inevitable is inevitable, and I'm more a man of lyrics than melody.

The End of the Tunnel is the Beginning of the Light

Not ordinary or extraordinary, not
Normal or abnormal, not intelligent or
Idiotic, not handsome, not ugly

Blah
Blah blah—not anything, oh
Really?

I begin to conspire a rebuttal against
The proposed non-meaning of my "miserable" existence
BUT

Such a rebuttal
Would last until
My death

So instead
I stare
At my hands

And though I don't
See much, I don't see the rebuttal, and
The little I do see means more to me

I
Like my
Fingernails

Which are
Currently quite long
Actually, and

Soon, I'm not sure
When, but soon
I'll trim my fingernails

The Beach Scene

On occasion I want something
Until I have it, and then I regret

Having wanted it. On occasion I
Write a line that doesn't refer

To the previous line. On occasion
I'm trying to flee from a previous

Line. On occasion I'm wanting to find
A way to flee from myself. You know,

I used to treat the epigraph to Sam
Shepard's *The One Inside* seriously, its

David Foster Wallace quote, "Why
Does no one take you outside and

Tell you what is coming?" But now
I consider that question hilarious.

Have you ever tried to tell someone
What life feels like? And when you

Told them, did they know what to do
With that information? Well, for me

Personally, my feelings are
Abstractions, accidental secret

Riddles that make people scratch
Their noggins if anything. Exactly.

<u>If I Want to I Should</u>
<u>a.k.a Maybe I Am Concentrating</u>

Part One

Well, I wake up and I feel as if
Life is typical. I have myself a

Reasonable perspective and I
Understand a world that

Makes sense after I concentrate.
Although I'm still, um, fucked.

Part Two

The near distant
Seems super distant.

Since 2020
Lasted a decade.

And now my childhood
Never actually transpired.

Part Three (Flashback)

I am on a deserted city street during a curfew
Following neighborhood BLM protests and

I am on a date, holding a phone that faces
Me, wearing headphones and drinking

A beer my other hand holds. Tonight I am
On a video date that takes place over phones,

And drinking beer on deserted city streets.
2020: Come to me and leave me alone.

Part Four

My buddy from high school is turning
'Publican, so when I bring up UBI with him

Well, the convo becomes about not robots
But welfare, and he goes off on a tangent.

You see: a UBI might be necessary
After robots replace us, but anyway.

At one point, I forget why, he says the
Government will start another pandemic.

As if our own pandemic has been a
Government plan, I mean, are you certain?

Part Five

Next, January 2021: Trump is gone but the
Plague continues, and honestly even though

The plague isn't new, and there's a fresh
President, still I didn't quite anticipate the

Miserable feelings of this month, because
One point is, and there are multiple points,

One point is some things you have to
Experience before you know how they feel.

Reacting to Driving Across Sunset Strip on a Wednesday Night

Sunset Strip, its lights and its buildings
The inside of me, my writing

The Marvel Cinematic Universe
The Shawn Michael Sullivan Literary Universe

Over seven-and-a-half billion people
And I am one of them

Thousands of years of human existence
And this is my one life

Billions more people will be born and
Billions of years will still transpire

But only one of me
And for a little while

There are many other cities and
Only one West Hollywood

Plenty of other city streets but
This is Sunset Strip

<u>Someone knocks over something in the background</u>

And it is loud

Right when I was making the greatest statement
I had ever made.

Which I wouldn't have stated if not
For what Wendy had said.

Sometimes I say the right thing
At the wrong time.

And sometimes I say the wrong thing
At the right time.

But I never get the right and
Wrong to coincide.

Of course, how is that
Related to avocados?

Please, More Like Apostrophes

Wendy, you're fine
And I'm fine too.

We both think you're fine
And I think I am too.

Wendy, can you hear me?
What I am trying to say is

This is all I am. So okay
Wendy, Wendy, if you can

Hear me, what I am getting at
Is, since this is all of me

What about this. And
I don't think you'd say

This Isn't a World of Excuses

The me who knows everything is going
Terribly is friends with the me who knows

It doesn't matter. That second me means to say
That a lot more people know what's best in life

Than are what's best in life.
Origami, oh, origami!

And both of me know to pay my taxes
Though a third me can't believe this shit

Any shit, can't believe none of it.
A fourth me stays quiet because one

Should choose one's fights they say.
Although the whole world deserves a fight

I say, and just part of me stays quiet,
But not because the world feels right.

Flaneur Stuff From a Los Angeles Perspective

On sidewalks I wear out the soles
Of my shoes, the heels of my shoes, and
The general condition of my shoes.

Wherever I walk I search for shadows,
Always, to avoid the sun that thrives in an
Immense blue sky above me. Walking is

Not that complicated and I am an expert.
I am an expert at walking specifically. I know
More about walking than anything else. Oh,

I observe some buildings and whatnot.
Businesses, banks and et cetera exist. I see
Them. Bunch of other people. Cars. Honk.

Miscellaneous city noises transpire, and the
Street smells. That guy smells. There is a
Billboard, right here. And the tick-tock of

The clock exists most of all. As I stroll a
Sidewalk the calendar pages turn, and I walk
Through a city to make it through a day.

Classic Movie Scenes Play Behind My Eyelids

A staircase behind her front door leads to her
Apartment, and I have brought along two cans

Of White Claw that I consider charming, although
They won't charm this high school art teacher

Who drinks red wine and sings me a song from
The musical *Oliver!* I adore the singing of this

Woman whose pussy I eat while *The Great British
Baking Show* plays on her tiny tv across the room.

Paintings on her walls, she is something of a painter
Herself. Note: the two kittens she adopted once

Quarantine began. We bathe together and sleep
Together, she cooks breakfast and I stay another

Evening, leave in the second morning—then never
See her again. In our best moments we called

Ourselves an apocalyptic romance, lovers in a cabin.
She had asked if I'd write about her, and I told her

I'm sure I'll remember when she said I'm not
Husband material. And she gave me a look that

Indicated she wanted to be remembered for more.
Well, I did write more about her. She gave up

On me but I didn't give up on our poem.
And I still remember: *Who will buy my*

*Sweet red roses? Any milk today, Mistress?
Two blooms for a penny. Ripe strawberries, ripe!*

www.ingramcontent.com/pod-product-compliance
Lightning Source LLC
Chambersburg PA
CBHW020445030426
42337CB00014B/1397